Get Set For Fun

Written by David Lavelle

Collins

T0321824

Get set! Put on boots.

Pack a map in a rucksack.

March up a hill. Go back down!

Go up a ladder.

Run in the rain.

Look for earwigs in the moss.

Dip for fish in rock pools.

Set up a den at sunset.

Hear owls hoot in the dark.

See bats by torchlight.

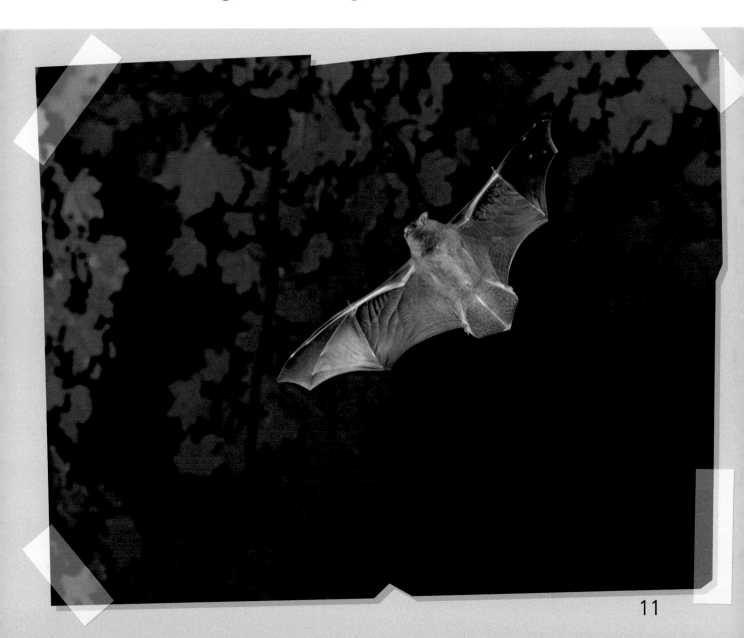

Cook food at night.

See the moon.

Get set
boots ✓
map ✓

In the sun
hill ✓
ladder ✓

In the wet
rain ✓
earwigs ✓
rock pools ✓

At night
den ✓
food ✓
moon ✓

15

After reading

Letters and Sounds: Phase 3

Word count: 61

Focus phonemes: /ow/ /oo/ /ar/ /ee/ /ear/ /or/ /er/ /igh/ /ai/ */oo/*, dd

Common exception words: go, by, the, put

Curriculum links: Understanding the world: The world

Early learning goals: Listening and attention: children listen attentively in a range of situations; Understanding: answer 'how' and 'why' questions about their experiences and in response to stories or events; Reading: read and understand simple sentences, use phonic knowledge to decode regular words and read them aloud accurately, read some common irregular words

Developing fluency

- Your child may enjoy hearing you read the story.
- You could take turns to read a page. Model reading with lots of expression and encourage your child to do the same.

Phonic practice

- Practise reading multi-syllable words together. Look at the word **torchlight** together. Ask your child to sound talk and blend the letter sounds in each syllable 'chunk': torch/light
- Do the same with the following words:

  sun/set   ruck/sack   ear/wigs

Extending vocabulary

- Ask your child if they can tell you the opposite word (antonym) for each of the following:

  night (day)   dark (light)   up (down)   on (off)